Assembly Rescue Service

Assembly Rescue Service

ALL THE HELP YOU NEED

Rob Hurd

kevin
mayhew

First published in 2003 by
KEVIN MAYHEW LTD
Buxhall, Stowmarket, Suffolk, IP14 3BW
Email: info@kevinmayhewltd.com

© 2003 Rob Hurd

The right of Rob Hurd to be identified as the author of this work has been asserted by him in accordance with the Copyright, Designs and Patents Act, 1988.

No part of this publication may be reproduced, stored in a retrieval system, or transmitted, in any form or by any means, electronic, mechanical, photocopying, recording or otherwise, without the prior written permission of the publisher.

All rights reserved.

9 8 7 6 5 4 3 2 1 0

ISBN 1 84417 013 6
Catalogue No. 1500563

Cover design by Angela Selfe
Edited and typeset by Elisabeth Bates

Printed and bound in Great Britain

Contents

Acknowledgements	7
About the author	9
Introduction	11
Go for it . . .	13
Learning from our mistakes	15
You have the potential	17
Image	19
Face value	24
How we treat others	27
I love . . .	31
Anger	34
Friendship	36
Following the crowd	40
What a mess . . .	43
Consequences	46
The solution!	48
Heroes	50
Stand up!	54
I name you . . .	57
Dear Lord . . .	59
Trust	62
Fears	64
Advice	66
Cars	69
Ziggy	72
This world	75

Harvest	77
Mothers...	80
The cost of love (Easter)	83
All smashed up (Easter)	85
Stuff the turkey (Christmas)	87
The reason for the season (Christmas)	90
Can you believe it? (Christmas)	92

Acknowledgements

Thanks to...

Jesus for giving me a sense of humour, a desire to have fun, and the opportunity to use both these throughout the years in different school assemblies, lunchtime and after-school clubs, and youth and children's clubs.

Also for inspiring and anointing me so that I could write the various poems and sketches and use them as a tool for telling children and teenagers about the difference Christ can make in their lives, and enabling them to think about the issues that relate to them.

Julie Hurd for her contribution to the book, being loving and supportive over the years, and listening to all the poems, sketches and rap songs I've tried out on her! (over and over again).

The various schools for their support and for allowing us to try out new assemblies.

About the author

Rob Hurd has worked for 11 years as a schools worker and youth worker. He worked in Lutterworth, Leicestershire for two years from September 1989 to 1991. He set up and ran a schools team called 'Lifeline', regularly visiting all the junior and secondary schools in the area to take assemblies, and he ran two Christian Unions. He also worked as a council youth worker and church youth/children worker at that time, organising a variety of youth events and missions.

In 1993 he started working for 'In Christ in School' as a secondary school worker and youth worker, regularly visiting 20 middle and upper comprehensive schools to take assemblies, lessons, and lunchtime and after-school clubs. He also organises a youth weekend each year called 'Spotlight' in which he and a team of volunteers take away approximately 100 young people to Derbyshire for a whole range of activities. He runs youth clubs, organises and speaks at youth events, churches, holiday clubs and school workers' meetings.

Rob Hurd can be contacted at robjhurd@hotmail.com

Introduction

As a schools worker and youth worker with 11 years of experience, I fully understand the pressures that other schools and youth workers face.

Finding good-quality material and resources can be difficult. Finding time to prepare for an assembly or talk can be even harder. The great benefit that this book offers is that all the material has been tried and tested many times over the last 11 years, and will work well!

The other great benefit is that it requires very little preparation. This book is geared for those who need good ideas, but have little time to prepare. You can pick up this book and use it for an assembly or talk almost straight away!

Go for it...

Aim

The aim is to show that if you're committed to achieving something, and give it your full energy, then you may be able to achieve more than you could ever imagine.

Equipment

A chocolate bar
Flipchart or piece of card

Outline

Introduction
Produce a bar of chocolate and explain how gorgeous chocolate is. Talk about how great it would be to be the manager of a chocolate factory! Then read out the chocolate bar sketch below.

'If I were...'
Imagine... if I were the boss of a big chocolate factory... Mmm, imagine that...

I'd be really intelligent, a real *smartie*. I'd do really well and be very successful. I'd have to give talks on chocolate making, and I'd always get an *applause*, and be the *topic* of everyone's conversation. In fact, life would be a bed of *roses*.

I'd make loads of money, have a nice house in *Quality Street*, a nice big car and I'd be able to take *time out* to go on expensive holidays to the Bahamas! I'd have *picnics* on the beach and the occasional *twirl* at the local beach disco; yeah, life would be great, full of pleasant *moments*. I'd be one of those *strollers* through life. In fact, life would be one constant *whirl*, with plenty of *celebrations*.

Then I would retire, get my *bounty*, a massive pension – that's *good news*. Eventually I would *flake* out, but at least I would have had a good life. I wonder, what's the *secret*? Oh, to be rich and successful.

If I said I was rich, I'd be *lion*, but I can dream. It gives me a bit of a *boost*. I might not be a manager of a chocolate bar factory but I'm OK. I had my mind in another *orbit* while I was at school, I liked to play *twix* on my mates and mess about. I was a bit of a *bandit*, so I didn't get many good marks. I wasn't into *clubs*, but life's not been too bad. I've had a few *crunchies* in life, been a bit of a *drifter*. Life's more like one long *marathon* – hard work! I don't know about the Bahamas. I went off to Skeggy last year with my mate *Bertie Bassett* and his little *yorkie*. We had a *Double Decker*, it was OK.

Life is good, and I have my dreams... if I were...

ASSEMBLY RESCUE SERVICE

Illustrations
Ask the group to shout out things that they would like to achieve this year. Write them down on a piece of card or flipchart.

Explain about how difficult some things are to achieve – you need to be really committed to succeed – but say that even though some things may seem impossible they can be achieved.

Give some examples of people who have broken world records (try to use funny examples – you'll find some in the *Guinness Book of Records*) and mention how the challenges seemed impossible, but they tried their best and succeeded. We also need to encourage each other to achieve certain things in life. Here are some examples:

- Janusz Chomatek of Poland bounced a tennis ball on his head for 105 minutes. He bounced it 15,225 times (145 bounces a minute).
- The longest single unbroken apple peel on record is one of 172 feet 4 inches peeled by Kathy Wafler aged 17 of Wolcott, New York. It took her 11 hours 30 minutes to do in October 1976.
- The longest recorded duration for balancing on one foot is 33 hours by U. S. Kumar Anando of Sri Lanka in May 1980.
- Don Cooke of Ohio, USA, had 21,000 bees swarm around him, and rest on his neck and chest in June 1980.
- The fastest barber on record shaved 368 men in 60 minutes.
- Erol Bird yodelled non-stop for 10 hours 15 minutes in October 1979.
- John Massis or 'Hercules' from Belgium raised a weight of 233 kg (513 5/8 lbs) 5 inches from the ground in March 1977, with his teeth!! Apparently he also prevented a helicopter from taking off using just a teeth harness in Los Angeles in 1979.
- Matthew McGregory had the world's biggest feet – 18 inches!! He wore size 26 shoes and they cost £1500 a pair. Not bad for a man 7ft 4 inches tall (and 21 stone in weight).
- In 1979 David Donoghue dropped fresh eggs 650 feet from a helicopter onto a Tokyo golf course. The eggs didn't break.

Bible bit
Tell the story of Noah and how he achieved something great by building the ark, in spite of it being difficult and everyone laughing at him. However, his commitment, and faith in God, proved him right.

Conclusion
Finish by saying that if we ask for God's help, and trust in him for the right things, then he can give us the ability to achieve great things.

Learning from our mistakes

Aim

To show that we all make mistakes and we do things that we know are wrong. The Bible calls this sin. The aim is to show that we need to learn from our mistakes, and that Jesus died for us so that we could be forgiven.

Equipment

Juggling balls or clubs
Water pistol or gong

Outline

Introduction

Ask if anyone has ever made any mistakes. Then tell the story about Jimmy who made lots of mistakes.

Jimmy and his...

This is a story about a man called Jimmy who was a carpet fitter, a bad carpet fitter. In fact, he was so bad that business was terrible. You see, he made mistakes, like getting the measurements wrong, and ending up with holes in the wrong places, and cutting round heavy furniture instead of moving it, leaving a big hole when the furniture was moved. So he didn't have much work, until one day an old lady rang him up and asked him to do a big job at her house...

When he got there he found that it was a large mansion owned by the lady, and it wasn't just a carpet, it was a *big* carpet. Fifty feet long and twenty feet wide. It took hours to lay it. 'No mistakes,' he thought. He was proud of his work.

Finally he'd finished. 'Time for a cigarette,' he thought. He hadn't had one all day' so he reached into his jacket pocket. Oh funny, I thought my cigarettes were in there; I must have left them in the van.' He looked in the van, under the dashboard, but they were nowhere to be seen.

As he went back inside he saw the old lady coming down the hallway with a nice cup of tea. Suddenly he stopped in horror. As he turned round he saw a large lump under the carpet, right in the middle! Quickly he ran to his tool bag and got out his hammer. With two quick, heavy thumps he squashed the lump down, just as the old lady came in with a cup of tea and said, 'Jimmy, I've made you a cup of tea, and I found your cigarettes – have you seen my pet hamster?'

Illustrations

Explain that we all make mistakes and say yes to doing wrong when we should say no, and we say no to doing right when we should say yes.

Then play the game 'Yes/No' with two volunteers and ask them questions. They can say anything but yes or no – either sound a gong or squirt them with a water pistol if they make a mistake.

Try juggling with some balls or juggling equipment, explaining that the number one rule for juggling is to learn from your mistakes, and in the same way we should learn from our mistakes in life.

Bible bit

Tell the story about Zacchaeus (Luke 19).

Conclusion

Finish by saying that when we do wrong or sin God hates it, yet the most important thing that we, as Christians believe, is that Jesus died for our sins so that we can be forgiven. Like Zacchaeus, we can have a relationship with God by accepting Jesus Christ as our Lord.

You have the potential

Aim

To show that everybody has a gift and ability; however, so often we try to be something or someone we're not, but God loves us as we are.

Equipment

Five household bricks

Outline

Introduction

Get six volunteers to come up to the front. Split the rest of the group into two teams. Ask three of the volunteers to stand in front of one team and the other three in front of the other. Give one volunteer from each team a famous character and they both have to act it out to their team. The team that guesses correctly wins a point. Then give the next two volunteers another famous character each.

Mention that the whole game is about acting out a famous character. Explain that very often in life people try to be something or someone they're not. They try to act tough when they want to cry or be accepted. They look up to famous pop or film stars (and dream about being them) but God loves them for who they are, not who they would like to be. He sees what they're like and loves them.

Illustration

Mention how many amazing things we can do in this life – we can achieve so much. Read out these 'vital statistics'. The average person will, in a lifetime:

- Spend three-and-a-half years eating.
- Grow 28 yards of fingernails and 450 miles of hair on the head.
- Talk on the phone for two-and-a-half years.
- Walk 13,673 miles.
- Produce 200 billion new red blood cells (every day), 70,385 pints of urine and spend more than six months on the loo.
- Shed 45 lbs of dead skin.
- Be able to name 2000 people and call 150 of them friends.

- Have dribbled 145 litres of saliva by the age of 12 months and by the age of 2 will have crawled an average of 80 miles.
- Have had about 368 million heartbeats in 10 years.
- By the age of 21, have breathed enough air to fully inflate 3.5 million balloons.
- Grow more than 6 feet of nose hair.
- Learn how to distinguish between 10 million colours.
- Talk for 12 years.
- Kiss for 2 weeks.
- Blink their eyes 415 million times.

Bible bit

Tell the story of Noah (Genesis 7) who built this amazing ark – against all the odds.

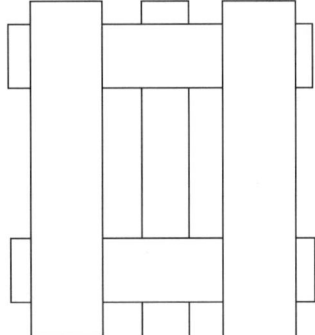

Illustration

Produce the five household bricks and ask if there is a volunteer who can pick up all five bricks with one hand. When no one can do the trick you lay one brick on its side, put two bricks on their side at either end of the brick, then lay another two bricks either end of these bricks. Put your hand in the middle, hold the bottom brick and pick up the five bricks.

Conclusion

Finish by saying that everyone has a gift or ability and even though a situation may seem impossible, like the brick trick, God can help us to achieve great things like Noah.

Image

Aim

'If you want to be accepted, then you need the right image'. This is often the philosophy that people have, especially young people. Advertising plays a large part in this and can put a lot of pressure on young people to have the right image as far as looks, clothing, lifestyle and attitude are concerned.

Whilst these things may seem important, the aim of this theme is to put across the idea that having the right image isn't the most important thing; it's what a person is like on the inside that matters. Also, God loves us, and sees us as precious, no matter what we are like on the outside.

Equipment

Sketchboard and pens

Outline

Introduction

Start by saying that some adverts are really good, and give an example of a good advert. Talk briefly about how advertisers often use captions or rhymes to advertise their products.

Guess the ad

Play this Quiz by reading out the captions and get the group to guess which product is being sold.

- There's nothing quite like ... *McDonald's*™
- The best a man can get ... *Gillette*™
- Take two bottles into the shower? Not me, I just ... *Wash 'n' Go*™
- Just do it ... *Nike*™
- To be this good takes ages ... *Sega*™
- I'll bet he drinks ... *Carling Black Label*™
- If you like a lot of chocolate on your biscuit join our ... *Club*™
- Do you love anyone enough to give them your last ... *Rolo*™
- Somebody cares ... *Boots*

- Wherever there is fun there's always ... *Coca Cola*™
- You know when you've been ... *Tango*™
- The jeans that built America ... *Levi's*™
- Everything we do is driven by you ... *Ford*™

Write on the sketchboard the word 'Image', and say that advertising is all about image. Four important aspects are LOOKS, APPEARANCE, LIFESTYLE and ATTITUDES.

Write the words and as you write each one give examples of TV adverts to back you up, for instance:

LOOKS – talk about adverts on television for men's aftershave, or ladies' perfumes, or tights, where they use beautiful, slim girls, or tough, good looking men.

APPEARANCE – explain how people who star in TV adverts always wear nice expensive clothes or designer gear.

LIFESTYLE – mention that adverts for washing powder or cereals, often show large, tidy houses in nice suburban areas.

ATTITUDES – explain that advertisers often put across the image that being wealthy and competitive in life is good.

After you have written and talked about those four different aspects on the sketchboard, relate them to young people and how it affects them.

LOOKS – there is so much pressure on young people, especially girls, to look good. The attitude is that they need to be slim and beautiful if they want to get anywhere in life. This is portrayed all the time on adverts and television. Although this is not quite as strong for males, there is still that pressure to look tough.

APPEARANCE – 'You should only wear trainers with brand names. You need to be fashionable to be accepted.' This seems to be the attitude that's often put over to young people.

LIFESTYLE – there is a lot of pressure on young people to follow the crowd; they can't be seen to be different. If their friends are smoking, taking drugs or drinking alcohol, then they feel they should try it, as they don't want to be picked on for being soft or boring.

ATTITUDES - again it's easier for young people to go along with their friends concerning attitudes towards things such as belief, moral values, or behaviour.

Write the word ACCEPTANCE on the board, and say that we will do almost anything to be accepted.

```
┌─────────────────────┐
│      IMAGE          │
│                     │
│                     │
│                     │
│   ACCEPTANCE        │
└─────────────────────┘
```

Introduce the rap 'Face it' by saying that the character would do anything to be accepted, but in the end it was all about image - was that enough?

Face it
You gotta be cool
   when you go to school.
You gotta look the part
   and dress alright,
   be OK, hang out at night.

Do the right thing,
   take the right stuff;
   one of the gang,
   act real tough.
Follow the crowd,
   don't be loud,
   just do as we say
   and go our way.

Morals are out,
   religion's not cool,
   stuff authority -
   we follow no rule.

Life's a race,
>   we're on our own, no one matters.
>
> We follow no code –
>   live for yourself,
>   stuff the rest
>   do what you want
>   ignore the mess.

But when you're alone,
>   no one but you,
>   you think about life
>   and what you've been through.
>
> What's it about?
> Why are we here?
> I feel sad and lonely,
>   don't shed a tear.

Why am I hurt, so unloved,
>   misunderstood, never hugged?
>
> I look on the wall
>   and see the cross –
>   Jesus died, and I didn't give a toss.
>
> Could he fill the gap?
> Could he give me life?
> Take away the hurt,
>   get me outta strife?

Could he love me now, as a dad,
>   look at my heart
>   and ignore the bad?
>
> Forgive me, love me,
>   set me free?
>
> Could I follow God?
> I'd like to see.

If only . . .

Conclusion

Finish by saying that at the end of the day image isn't that important! It doesn't matter what we look like, how we dress or what we own. We should never judge others by what they look like on the outside and always respect each other's beliefs and attitudes.

Also explain that God made us as we are. We are all special, and he loves us, as with the rap 'Face it'. He doesn't care what we look like on the outside, but what we are like on the inside.

Face value

Aim

To show that we often judge people purely on face value, instead of seeing what they're like as individuals. Young people need to see the value in each other. Also, as they go through life, some situations may seem bad on the surface but there is a God who cares for them.

Equipment

3-D poster
Magic bag (available from all magic shops) containing some dead and some live flowers OR
a tin of stew with a cat-food label stuck over the stew label

Outline

Introduction

Hold up a 3-D poster and ask for a volunteer to see if they can see the 3-D picture. Explain the difficulty in seeing what the picture is meant to be. Use a lot of humour and go through the process in which you discover the picture, i.e. going cross-eyed or bending over to look straight at it.

Explain that on the surface the poster looks confusing and weird, and you can't understand what it is meant to be, yet if you manage to see through the pattern you will find a lovely picture.

In the same way we often take people at face value and judge them because we can't understand them or they look different or weird, rather than seeing what they're really like as individuals. Read out the rap below.

Face it
You gotta be cool
    when you go to school.
You gotta look the part
    and dress alright,
    be OK, hang out at night.

Do the right thing,
    take the right stuff;
    one of the gang,
    act real tough.
Follow the crowd,
    don't be loud,
    just do as we say
    and go our way.

Morals are out,
    religion's not cool,
    stuff authority –
    we follow no rule.
Life's a race,
    we're on our own, no one matters.
We follow no code –
    live for yourself,
    stuff the rest
    do what you want
    ignore the mess.

But when you're alone,
    no one but you,
    you think about life
    and what you've been through.
What's it about?
Why are we here?
I feel sad and lonely,
    don't shed a tear.

Why am I hurt, so unloved,
    misunderstood, never hugged?
I look on the wall
    and see the cross –
    Jesus died, and I didn't give a toss.
Could he fill the gap?
Could he give me life?
Take away the hurt,
    get me outta strife?

Could he love me now, as a dad,
   look at my heart
    and ignore the bad?
Forgive me, love me,
   set me free?
Could I follow God?
I'd like to see.

If only . . .

Bible bit
Tell the story of when Jesus was anointed by Mary Magdalene, the prostitute (Luke 8:36–50). Everyone thought of her as disgusting, yet Jesus loved her for what she was like as a person.

Illustration
Produce the magic bag and fill it with dead flowers, and show how, if you look further, amazingly, they have come back to life. Explain that you may feel like dead flowers but God doesn't see you like that. He sees life in you, he loves you and sees you as very precious.

   If you haven't got a magic bag then produce the 'cat food' tin and offer it to any volunteers to eat. When no one comes to eat some, start eating the 'cat food' yourself.

Conclusion
Finish by saying that although the label says 'cat food' it is really stew. So the message is, don't judge people by what they're like on the outside – it's what's *inside* that matters!

How we treat others

Aim

To encourage the group to think about how they treat other people in life. We need to treat people with respect and dignity. Also, God still sees us as special no matter how people, or life, treats us.

Equipment

A £5 or £10 note
Flipchart and two pens

Outline

Introduction

Ask for two volunteers to come to the front. Give each of them a different coloured marker pen. Ask them to write on the flipchart as many types of jobs where people care for others as they can think of. The rest of the group can shout out things to help the volunteers. After a minute see who has written the most things on the chart. Give the loser a big bar of chocolate and the winner a penny sweet.

Explain that the game was all about caring for other people – and yet the winner only got a penny sweet and the loser got a big bar of chocolate. Ask if that sounds fair, then give the winner a bar of chocolate as well, and explain that in life we should always treat people fairly and with respect. If we treat people badly, we may lose people's friendship and love.

Read out the poem below:

I'll sort you out
Huh, look at that lad in my school,
    I can't stand him, he's a fool.
Thinks he's great, thinks he's alright,
    I'd love to punch him and start a fight.
He's good at maths, it makes me sick,
    he looks at me just like I'm thick.
The girls all like him, they think he's sound,
    wherever he goes they're all around.

He dresses smart and always got money,
> everyone thinks that he's so funny.
So tonight I'll put him right in his place,
> kick him and punch him in the face . . .

As for work it's not so bad,
> apart from the boss, who's really sad.
He works so hard, he's in a race,
> moaning and groaning, on our case.
No time for breaks, no time to shirk.
That boss is stupid – he makes us work.
'Be on time and work hard!' he'll shout,
> 'or if you skive my lad, you're out.'
Work hard for him, it makes me rage,
> except I like the nice big wage.
But I'd love to put him in his place,
> kick him and punch him in the face . . .

Out on the town every night,
> I work hard, so it's my right.
Gambling and drinking, enjoying life,
> better than being at home with the wife.
She cares for the kids and cooks my food,
> I'll put her straight if she's in a mood.
Life's for living, so enjoy it now,
> so long as I'm OK, it don't matter how.
If anyone gets in my way
> I'll sort them out, I'll make them pay.
So mess with me, and you will see,
> I'd love to put you in your place,
> kick you and punch you in the face . . .

A whole load of rubbish over the garden wall,
> that'll teach them for nicking my ball.
That Beryl and Derek, the miserable pair,
> moaning and groaning – it isn't fair.
Turn on the music late at night,
> bang on the wall and give them a fright.
Let down their tyres and spit on the cat,
> throw dog poo on their front doormat.

Serves them right for being so posh,
>   looking at me and saying 'oh gosh'.
I'll teach them a lesson they'll remember well,
>   don't mess with me, I'm the neighbour from hell . . .

Huh, Happy Christmas, so they say,
>   so what's the point of Christmas Day?
Presents, food, and family round,
>   so why can't I hear a sound?
The wife has left – the kids have gone,
>   no cards for me, not even one.
No food or presents, no one but me,
>   sad and alone – why couldn't I see,
>   all my life I've been full of hate
>   and now alone it's much too late.
My boss, my mates, my kids and wife,
>   I've treated them bad all my life.

Revenge is sweet – so they say,
>   but that's why I'm so alone today.
What's my future, so full of fears,
>   why can't I stop the flood of tears?

Too late . . .

Why? . . .

Conclusion

Finish by holding up the £5 or £10 note and saying that God sees us as precious as the money, yet:

- Some people in life may hate you (spit on the note and say that spitting on someone is a way of showing hatred to them).
- Some people may call you names, and you can feel crushed (crush the note in your hand).
- Some people may do things to you which are really bad, and you feel like you've been walked over (stamp on the note).
- Sometimes you may go through situations in life that make you feel torn apart (rip the note in half down the middle).

BUT, the note which has been spat on, crushed, stamped on and torn apart is still worth £5 or £10. It has kept its value. You can change it at any bank or shop because it hasn't lost its value at all! (Don't sue me if it doesn't work – it worked for me.)

Explain that in the same way people may treat you badly and you may go through terrible situations in life, but you are still valuable to God no matter what.

I love . . .

Aim

To show that romantic 'gooey' love often has no depth and requires little sacrifice, compared to agape love which is eternal, sacrificial and life-changing.

Equipment

Sketchboard
Marker pens
Valentine's card (or a gooey birthday card)
Bible

Outline

Introduction

Produce a valentine's card and talk about any romantic experiences you've had. Mention that love can be 'gooey' and how there are many different symbols which depict love.

Sketchboard

On the sketchboard fill in the word 'love' and ask the group for different symbols to do with love. If anyone is good at drawing ask them to draw the different symbols. If not, draw the symbols on the board yourself. Some good examples are:

SWALK – sealed with a loving kiss

HOLLAND – hope our love lasts and never dies

FLOWERS/CHOCOLATES

KISSES

HEART with an arrow through it.

Mention that kisses are the most important symbols as they are always on the end of a love letter or valentine's card and carry much more meaning than ending with 'yours faithfully'.

LOVE

Explain that this 'gooey' love requires little sacrifice, has little depth and therefore doesn't always satisfy, whereas real love is very tough.

Bible bit
Read 1 Corinthians 13:4–7. Love is patient…

Explain that real love is hard, as shown in the Bible text, but the test of real love is sacrifice. Ask if anyone would be willing to die for somebody else.

We need to love each other by being nice to each other and helping each other – that would make the world a better place to live. After the discussion, read out the story below.

The miners' story
It was winter. The miners got into the rickety old minibus to be taken back down the mountain to their warm homes. It had been raining, and the brakes were a bit dodgy, but the miners didn't mind. The driver was careful, and there was never any other traffic on the mountain road, so they set off down the winding road that would take them to their village. On their left was the steep mountain wall and on their right was a sheer drop, with the river at the bottom on the valley floor. They were driving along happily, and gathering speed. As they came round a sharp bend, suddenly to their horror they saw a small boy in the road. The driver had to make a split-second decision.

If he slammed on his brakes, the bus would skid and plunge all the miners to their death. He decided to continue and hoped that the boy would move out of the way in time. Sadly the boy didn't move in time and was killed.

When the driver managed to stop the vehicle he went up the hill to fetch the boy's body. The other miners were distraught and asked him why he couldn't avoid the boy, so he explained what the outcome would have been. If he'd turned left he would have hit the mountain wall and the boy. If he'd turned right he would have driven off the cliff edge and everyone would have been killed.

'Well, why didn't you sound the horn to warn the boy that we were coming?' they asked. The driver replied that to sound the horn would have been no good at all, because the child was deaf.

'How do you know?' they asked.

He looked at them with tears in his eyes and said, 'Because he was my only son.'

Conclusion

Finish by explaining that the most important symbols are the kisses, yet if you look at them from a different angle you will see that they are crosses.

Fill in the last word 'God' on the sketchboard and say that he loved us so much that he sent his Son Jesus to die for us. His HEART was pierced and he died on a cross.

NOW THAT'S REAL LOVE!

Anger

Aim

To show that sometimes we get angry at people, or because of situations we go through – but getting angry often makes the situation worse, and doesn't help us.

Equipment

Four balloons
Two pillows
A Bible

Outline

Introduction
Relate to the group a time when you lost your temper, and how it turned out, or tell a story about someone you know, or have read about, who lost their temper and how it worked out for them.

Game
Play the game 'Knock 'em down'. Ask for 2 volunteers; give them each a pillow. They have to stand on one leg and they have one minute to hit each other with the pillow (below the head). The loser is the one who puts their leg down first.

Explain that sometimes when people get angry they take it out on other people. When they go through problems it often makes them feel better by 'knocking others down' or hitting out at others.

Illustration
Produce the balloons:

- Take the first, blow it up fully and then burst it. Say that sometimes people get so angry they burst in a fit of temper and everyone knows about it.

- Blow up the second and let it go off into the air. Sometimes when people get angry, like the balloon they go everywhere, causing trouble.

- Blow up the third balloon and squeeze the end so that it makes a noise. Sometimes when people get angry they let everyone know about it and they can't keep quiet – they rant and rave and swear.

- Finally blow up the fourth balloon and put a knot into it. We should try to 'contain' our anger and not react like the other balloons

Conclusion

Finish by reading out these words from the Bible:

'[You] should be quick to listen, slow to speak, and slow to become angry, for your anger will not help you to live the right kind of life that God wants. When you are angry don't sin, and be sure to stop being angry before the end of the day.' (From James 1:19 and Ephesians 4:26.)

Encourage the group to try not to get angry but to talk to someone and explain what it is that is making them angry – they may be able to help. Walking away from a situation can sometimes help, but prayer is a way which many people undertake. If they're going through a problem they ask God for help and he takes away their anger.

Friendship

Aim

To show how important friendship is, and how we should love our enemies as much as ourselves.

Equipment

Disappearing hanky trick (or any trick where you can make an object disappear)

Outline

Introduction
Start by saying how important friendship is, or tell the following funny story to illustrate this.

Friend's advice
'Mmm, that smells nice,' thought the mouse as he sat in his hole in the wall. 'Lovely cheese.' He stuck out his nose to smell it. It was over there by the table in the living room. He ran out to get it, but as he did so he thought to himself, 'My friend told me to be aware of that devious, deceitful cat,' so he ran back in the hole. As soon as he got in, he heard the cat's miaow in the distance. He thought to himself, 'It's a good job I listened to my friend's advice. I'll wait till tomorrow to try and get it.'

The next day he woke up and smelt the lovely cheese again. Mmm lovely! He ran out to get it. Again he thought to himself, 'My friend taught me to be aware of that devious, deceitful cat.' As he ran back into his hole he heard the cat 'miaowing' in the distance. He thought to himself, 'It's a good job I listened to my friend's advice. I'll wait till later to get it'. Just then he heard a different noise in the background, a sort of 'woof! woof!' noise.

He thought to himself, 'Forget my friend's advice. If I run out and get the cheese the cat won't chase me, as he will be too concerned about the dog chasing after him!'

So the mouse ran out to get the cheese. He hadn't gone far when the cat pounced on him, and with one gobble ate him up. As the cat was cleaning his paws he thought to himself, 'I'm pleased I took my friend's advice and learned a second language. WOOF! WOOF!'

Explain how friendship is about being there for your friends, helping them out, being trustworthy, and wanting the best for them.

Magic trick

Before you do the magic trick wave the object about. Whilst doing that explain how some friends hang around with you, they're seen to be your friends, yet (make the object disappear), when you need them most they're gone!

Samaritan rap

Explain that this is based on the story of the Good Samaritan.

I was walking down the street just the other night,
    when I saw a gang of yobs and thought, 'Oh fright!'
They looked mean and they looked tough,
    not nice lads, a gang of roughs.
I looked at them,
    they looked at me.
Then I saw a smile full of glee.
I thought to myself,
    'They're going to chase me.'

So I started to run with all of my might,
    this looks bad – it's going to be tight.
Where could I run, I'd nowhere to go,
    I didn't see the nail enter my toe,
    with a cry of pain I hit the floor.
This is bad – how much more?

I can't remember much,
    just the first touch.
    'You're a wimp,' he said
    as he kicked my head.

I felt the pain,
    again and again,
    as he punched and hit,
    face full of wit,
    then I was pushed – into a pit.

How much more can I take?
I can't stand the human race!
As I lay in agony
    I saw an old lady pass by me.

'I'm hurt, can't you see?'
'Sorry my son – I'm off for tea!'

I saw a man walking past,
    I lifted my hand and said, 'Please help fast.'
He looked at me and said, 'You jerk!
    lying there, can't you work?'

The night was dark and very cold,
    both my arms I couldn't hold.
Will I die in this pit here?
Never seen – just disappear?
I still lay there in agony
    when I saw someone approaching me.
I heard 'em spit and loudly yell
    they looked like they'd come from hell.

The angel from hell didn't hesitate,
    he walked right up with his Hell's Angel mate.
They checked my pulse, it was OK.
'You'll be fine,' I heard them say.
They washed my wounds from water in a tub
    then carried me off to the local pub.

I lay on the bed resting my head,
    with food and drink causing a stink,
    but they didn't mind cos they were so kind.
My two biker mates had saved my life,
    came to help me, ending my strife.
They're keeping in touch,
    I owe them so much.
They're my mates, I could tell
    cos they saved me from a living hell.

A world with peace, without war,
    a place we want more and more.
So learn to love and not to hate,
    love your enemies, it's never too late.

Conclusion

Finish by saying how hard it is to forgive your friends when they let you down, but that it is an important part of friendship. Mention that the Bible talks about loving your enemies, as in the parable of the Good Samaritan. This is much harder, but if you can love your enemies the whole world would be a better place to live.

Following the crowd

Aim

To show that we are all followers of different things such as fashion trends and lifestyle. Most things that we follow aren't particularly bad for us, but they might not be necessarily good.

Equipment

Sketchboard
Marker pens
A prize for 'Simon says'

Outline

Introduction

Start by saying that we are all followers of different things. Sometimes we follow trends, or people, which can be harmless, but sometimes we follow things which we know can be dangerous for us.

Game

Choose about 10 volunteers from the group and play the game 'Simon says' (give the winner a prize).

Sketchboard

Fill in the words 'Follow the crowd'. Then explain that we are followers of certain things and give examples.

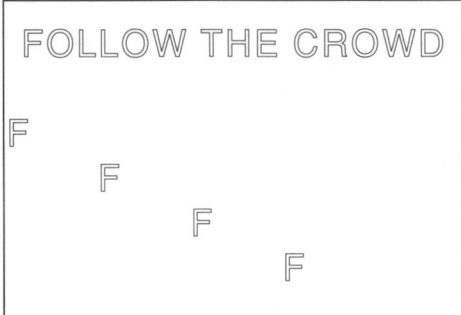

Fashion – styles of dress, hairstyles, designer labels . . .

Friends – peer pressure, attitudes to life, love and sex . . .

Fun – drugs, alcohol, smoking, etc.

False – cults, philosophies, harmful beliefs.

Ask if there are any good artists, and when you fill in the 'F' words ask them to draw an appropriate picture. When that is done, read out the sketch below.

Charlie

Hello, my name's Charlie. I don't have a second name, I'm just called Charlie.

I bet you're wondering what I do for a living. Well, whether you are or not, I'm going to tell you. Me, I'm no Bank Manager or anything like that, I'm too thick for that. You could say that I'm a bit SHEEPISH, really – that's a joke. Anymore like that and I'll be BAA-ED.

Me mam told me, 'EWE are stupid, good for nothing.' Well she was right, I am good for nothing. I don't do much and I don't get paid much either, so I guess I am good for nothing.

Have EWE guessed what I do? I'm a shepherd! 'Wow, what a job,' you're saying. I don't have much money, not a mint, sauce of money is zilch. You could say I work on the SHEEP; ha ha, that's another joke. Most people, when they can't sleep, try to count sheep in their minds. Me, I just look up.

But I do have a few adventures. Last week I was sitting on the hillside minding my own business, singing actually, or LAMB-ENTING you could say, ha ha. I looked at my sheep and sat upright, which is unusual for me, I tell you. I was in total shock, it was terrible, a catastrophe. Maybe I'm going on a bit, but I was quite surprised: Sweaty Betty was missing. I call her Sweaty Betty because she's called Betty, and she sweats a lot, you see.

Well, you might be saying, what with 100 sheep, how could I tell that one was missing? I'm not that thick, I can count up to 100, and I know all my sheep by name, plus the fact she's not called Sweaty Betty for nothing – anyone could tell she was missing – stinky old goat. I spend a lot of time with my sheep, so I know everything about them, even their toilet habits, especially that one Sue the Ewe with the smelly, well I don't need to get into that, unless I'm feeling cold that is.

Anyway, I searched high and low for Sweaty Betty, no good. So I left the other 99 sheep on their own, and went to look for her. I went across a river, down a valley and up a mountain. Eventually I found her, lazy goat. She'd stopped for a drink and got stuck in the mud; that was my adventure over. We got back to the others and had a party to celebrate; it was great. I was a bit suspicious though, we had shepherd's pie. Maybe they're trying to tell me something?

That's my job really, guiding the sheep to good pasture, none of this astro turf stuff, the real thing. Sometimes we play a game to amuse ourselves: it's called

'Follow the Leader'. It's a bit boring. We've been playing it for three years now, but I've not lost a sheep yet. Well, I keep a BAA chart. It's not always boring though, I had a bit of action last week. I had to chase Alfred the Wolf away, huh, greedy monster. I'm tough, you can call me BRUCE WOOLIES; nobody tries to take me on, that's why I'm a shepherd I suppose.

Anyway, I'm off on holiday next week, I bet you're wondering where I'm going – BAAbados, then BAAcelona of course.

Conclusion

Finish by explaining about the perfect shepherd who knows all his sheep by name, guides them to good pastures and protects them from harm. They follow him and trust in him.

Write the words 'Follow Jesus' on the sketchboard.

```
┌─────────────────────────┐
│                         │
│        FOLLOW           │
│                         │
│                         │
│         JESUS           │
│                         │
└─────────────────────────┘
```

Jesus is like the perfect shepherd. If we trust and follow him he will guide us through our lives and protect us. He knows everything about us and yet still loves us.

Isn't it better to follow Jesus rather than following the crowd?

What a mess . . .

Aim

To show that no matter how bad the world may seem, God is still in charge and instead of blaming him, we need to do our best to make the world a better place.

Equipment

Two balls of knotted string
Copy of 'Tragedy' by the Bee Gees

Outline

Introduction
Begin by reading out an article from a newspaper about some sort of tragedy that has happened recently. If there aren't any tell a story about a famous tragedy such as the terrorist attack on the World Trade Centre in September 2001 or of an earthquake disaster.

Game
Produce the balls of knotted string and ask for two volunteers. Give them each a ball and they have 30 seconds to see who can undo all the knots first.

Explain that the world is like the ball of string. Sometimes things go wrong along the way like the knots in the string. When there's a tragedy there seems to be no way out, and no way of getting through it, yet however bad a situation may seem, God is there and can help us if we put our trust in him. When the game is finished, read out the poem below.

Sad, bad and vile
Why worry about life?
Why fret all the time?
How can we cope?
All these problems – they're all mine.

Things don't go our way.
Life seems hard each day.

Stress at work, pressure to cope,
  stress at home, where's our hope?

Turn on the news, it's all so sad,
  violence, hatred, wars, murder,
  the world's so bad.
We feel lonely, hurtful, scared – so why
  does a loving God
  allow the world to die?

The children may suffer,
  they may share our pain,
  they may have problems,
  pressure and worries
  again and again.

BUT

I stop and pause just for a while,
  so this world is sad, bad and vile.
But whose fault is it anyway?
NOT God's but ours, our fault
  at the end of the day.

It could be so different,
  it could be great.
No wars but peace,
  no hatred but love.
God's plan, not fate.

No problems – but answers,
  no worries, doubts or fears,
  no sadness or crying, and no tears.

He died for us two thousand years ago.
On a cross he took our faults
  so we could know
  that life could be fine,
  laughter all the time.
Sharing and caring,

    living in unity,
    ignoring our differences,
    not just about me.

So the answer is Jesus,
    he's the only way.
He can make the difference
    in the world of today.
Forgive us, love us, and set us free,
    help us live life as it should be.

So if we say sorry and ask him in,
    in this world there would be no sin.
A nice place to live, a perfect creation,
    living as one – as God's holy nation.

Conclusion

End by asking the group to suggest different ways of making the world a better place to live. Some ideas could be giving to charity, taking part in charitable events, helping our neighbours, especially the elderly and being nicer to each other. When they've suggested some, encourage them to do their best to make the world a better place to live in.

Consequences

Aim

To show that often we do things that we know are wrong without thinking of the consequences. It's important to be aware that when we break the rules or sin, there is often a consequence.

Equipment

A conjuring trick (preferably a magic bag)
A flower (or bunch of flowers) and some dried-up flowers

Outline

Introduction
Produce either a chess or draughts board and ask if anyone plays. Talk about the game of chess, whenever you've played and lost. In the game when you move a piece, you never really know how each move will turn out. You can think you're doing well, and then lose.

Explain that as in chess, in life we never really know what the consequences of our actions will be. Read out some short true stories, in which the consequences are not quite what you would assume. (Steve Wright's book *Amazing But True* has many good examples.)

Alternatively read out an item from a newspaper and ask the group what they think the end is going to be (a funny story would be good, or a bad story).

Illusion
Perform a conjuring trick and go on to explain that with illusions you never know how it is going to turn out. When you have done the trick, read the following rap.

Hey, say no!
When you're feeling down,
    don't be a clown;
    don't ever take drugs
    cos that's for mugs!

You can get some weed
    and loads of speed,
    take smack and crack
    and your health you lack.

Don't try some coke
    or even smoke,
    cos in the end
    you're the joke.

When you're feeling sad
    remember drugs are bad,
    spend your money
    and you've been had.

There's a hole in your life
    you need to fill,
    Jesus Christ is the only pill.
With the Lord, you're all right,
    you got no worries,
    you can sleep at night.

He's the best
    so stuff the rest.
No bad thoughts, or ill effects
    with Jesus Christ everything checks.

Yo - drugs - SAY NO!!

Illustration

Hold up a bunch of flowers, and explain that this is how God considers you – very precious and special. But if you take or do things that you know are wrong, this is how you may end up – show some dried-up flowers. Explain that so many young people do things for fun, such as drug abuse, smoking or drinking without thinking about the consequences, which often can be fatal. These things can destroy you, as these flowers have been.

Conclusion

End by saying that we believe being a Christian is the best thing you can be and the only consequences are life in its fullness, a life with meaning and purpose, and eternal life in heaven.

The solution!

Aim

To show that however bad a situation may seem, there is often a solution. Also that God can help us with our problems.

Equipment

Eighteen long nails (one hammered into a piece of wood)
Any juggling equipment

Outline

Introduction

Start by telling a story about when things have gone disastrously wrong. It could be a personal or famous story (funny if possible).

Illustration

Produce some juggling equipment and talk about how difficult it is to juggle. Everything goes wrong, until you know what you're doing, then it becomes easier.

Bible bit

Tell the story of Jonah. Explain that everything went wrong, like the juggling, until he asked God to forgive him and was obedient.

Nail trick

Say that if the juggling seemed hard, this nail trick is even harder to do! Offer a box of chocolates to anyone who can balance 15 nails on top of one. When it can't be done do the trick yourself.

Show the single nail, nailed into a block of wood and ask if anyone can balance all 15 nails on top of it.

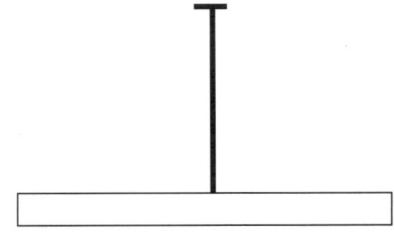

Can it be done?

THE SOLUTION is to lay one nail down on a flat surface, and rest the heads of the other 15 nails across it, half one way and half the other way. When that is done, then lay another nail between the heads of all the nails, pick them all up, and rest them on the nail, as below:

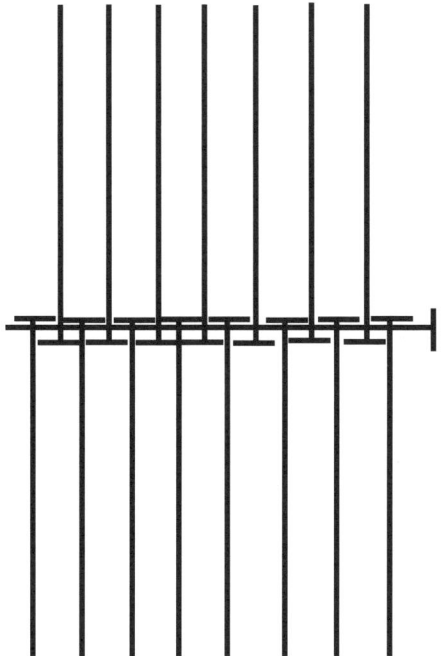

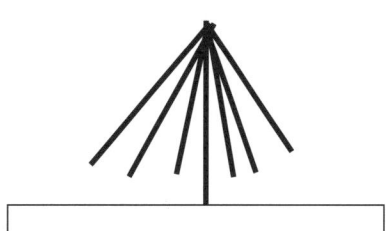

So you can now balance 15 (or more) nails on top of just one !!

Conclusion

End by explaining that we all have problems from time to time and our situations may seem really bad, but often there is a solution. It's important that we try to look for the solution. Explain that God is like the one nail. Just as it was possible to balance 15 nails on one nail, in the same way Christians believe that if we put our trust in God, he can help us through the difficult times in life, as he is the solution.

Heroes

Aim

To show that we all have heroes. In life there are many people we look up to, whether they are film stars, pop stars, sports stars or people we know personally, yet not many people would say that Jesus is a hero. By looking at Jesus we can see that he has all the characteristics of a hero!

Equipment

A magic trick (if you have one)
Sketchboard and pens

Outline

Introduction

If possible show a clip from a famous action film where the hero defies death and performs some great heroic stunt – could be a James Bond, Arnold Schwarzenegger or Batman/Superman film. Or you could describe a scene from a famous film where the hero performs a great death-defying stunt and then ask the assembly to guess which film it's from.

Explain that all great films have heroes in them. There are so many heroes on TV and in films.

Do the quiz 'Guess the Hero'.

Heroes Quiz

- This hero's catchphrase is 'shaken not stirred'. He likes gadgets and knows a secretary called Miss Moneypenny . . . *James Bond*
- This hero's catchphrase is 'with power comes great responsibility'. He's also not scared of heights . . . *Spiderman*
- This hero's catchphrase is 'to infinity and beyond'. His best mate is called Woody . . . *Buzz Lightyear*
- This hero hangs around in the forest and is in love with a maid . . . *Robin Hood*
- This hero's catchphrase is 'I'll be back'. Sometimes he's a hero, sometimes he's just evil . . . *Arnold Schwarzenegger*

- This man is the bravest man in Hollywood. He runs his own stunt performers' company and has had practically every bone in his body broken... *Jackie Chan*
- This hero's catchphrase is 'I'm just an ordinary cop who's in the wrong place at the wrong time'. He takes on bad guys, and wins everytime... *Bruce Willis*
- This hero's catchphrase is 'I am the way, the truth and the life'... *Jesus*
- This man can do everything really fast. He protects people and can fly... *Superman*
- This woman gave up everything to help people who were really poor. She lived in India... *Mother Teresa*

Sketchboard

Write on the sketchboard the word HEROES and ask everyone to think of as many heroes as possible such as pop/film/sports stars or people they know personally, then write them underneath.

Ask for characteristics of a hero and add them (i.e. tough, intelligent, kind, good-looking, daring).

Write the word Jesus on the sketchboard, then perform the rap below.

The hero

I was sitting on a wall,
   with no cares at all,
   enjoying the sun and resting my head
   when I heard a noise that could wake the dead.

Shouting and stamping loud and fast,
   thousands of people were running past.
People, people everywhere
   following some guy without a care.

There stood a man just like me
   but thousands were pushing just to see –

who was this guy with so much power?
He even made the Pharisees cower.

Some of the priests looked on in hate,
    the crowds loved Jesus, he was their mate.
The priests were jealous, it made them mad,
    with all their rules they made the people sad.

Follow the laws, keep them right,
    come to the Synagogue every night.
Do what we say, or else you pay,
    we'll treat you bad every day.

The crowds loved Jesus,
    he was God's Son,
    he taught them love
    and their hearts he won.

He raised the dead and healed the blind,
    helped some guy who'd lost his mind.
Walked on water, turned water to wine
    touched a leper and he was fine.

Everywhere he went, the crowds would go,
    he'd teach them things only God would know.
But then one night when he was out of sight
    he was arrested without a fight.

He was famous, the Big Boss,
    so why did he die on the cross?
'You're the King', his friends would say,
    so why did they all run away?

It was so sad, such a loss,
    to see a hero die on the cross.
But three days later he rose from the dead,
    went back to heaven, just like he said.

A real hero
Read out the points below then ask the group who they think the hero is.

This hero:

- Stood on the edge of a boat in a terrible storm, and stopped the storm by his command.
- Wrecked a marketplace, turning over the tables, letting animals free, without anyone laying a hand on him.
- Walked through hundreds of people while they tried to throw him off the edge of a cliff.
- Took on the devil and beat him.
- Brought dead people back to life, healed people, walked on water, and did loads of incredible miracles.
- Ensured that people who came to trap him and have him killed ended up going back to their bosses praising him.
- . Was constantly surrounded by thousands of people.
- Made really intelligent religious leaders look stupid when they tried to trick him.
- Died a terrible, violent death, rose from the dead and spent time with over 500 people during three weeks, and then rose up to heaven in front of his followers.

Conclusion

Finish by explaining that maybe Jesus wouldn't be classed as a hero in today's terms, maybe he would even be seen as a wimp for not answering back or fighting. Yet you can see he has all the characteristics of a real hero, and is the best hero anyone can have.

Stand up!

Aim

To encourage young people to stand up for what they believe to be right, especially concerning Christian and moral beliefs, but also to accept other people's beliefs and not to be prejudiced.

Equipment

Diablo
A testimony of someone who has stood up for their faith

Outline

Introduction

Have a go at a diablo or ask a volunteer to have a go and explain that it is all about control. Your hands control the sticks, the sticks control the string and the string controls the diablo, making it do certain things.

Talk about the fact that in the same way young people are a bit like that diablo. Young people are 'influenced' by peer pressure (string), peer pressure is controlled by the media – advertising on TV and magazines (sticks), the media is controlled by other people such as pop stars and fashion trends (hands). Often young people dress in the same style, do the same things, and have the same attitudes as their friends.

Rap

Introduce the rap below by saying that sometimes we just go along with other people rather than standing up for our own beliefs, but we also need to accept each other's beliefs and not be prejudiced even if we don't agree with them.

Stand up

When I was a baby I was small and cute,
    I crawled about in my new blue suit.
I felt quite sad and shed a tear
    cos in my world there was plenty to fear:
    tall things, sharp things, to be aware,
    I would be scared if my mum didn't care.

'Trust in God,' she would say,
    'read the Bible every day.
Talk to God, give him all your fears,
    walk with him and he'll dry your tears.'

Time for school, I can't be late,
    I need to go with my mate.
On my own I feel a mug
    and I get bullied by a thug.
He calls me names and picks on me,
    laughs and jokes for his mates to see.

'He's a weirdo,' the thugs would say,
    'goes to church every day,
    goody-goody Bible berk,
    prays to God, what a jerk!'

And my friends don't understand,
    they see me cry and don't lend a hand.
'Where's your God?' they'd say with hate,
    'trust in him if he's your mate.
God's no good – we don't care for him,
    all your faith is just a whim.
We don't need God – we're all right,
    mankind is the only might.'

On my knees I would shout,
'Please, Lord God, take away my doubt!'
The armour of God I would wear
    and I would know I'm in God's care.

'Trust in God,' Christ would say,
    'read the Bible every day.
Talk to God, give him all your fears,
    walk with him and he'll dry your tears.'

As I grew older, my heart grew colder,
    I knew what was wrong and what was right,
    but temptation blurred my spiritual sight.

My mates were bad, a bunch of thugs,
    they used to smoke and take drugs.
They would drink and sniff some glue
    and push it near for me to do.

Was I as bad as all the rest
    or was temptation just a test?
God was saying, 'Follow me,
    if you don't then you can flee.'

The choice was mine I had to make,
    follow God and my mates forsake.
Stand for God, be on his side
    or else to hell I would ride.

On my knees I will shout,
    'Please, Lord God, take away my doubt.'
YES!!!
The armour of God I will wear
    and now I know I'm in God's care.

Trust in God, Christ would say,
    read the Bible every day.
Talk to God, give him all your fears.
Walk with him and he'll dry your tears!

Conclusion

End by saying how we need to stand up for what we believe is right, especially regarding morals and Christian beliefs – just as in the rap – and give some examples of people who have stood up and been counted.

I name you . . .

Aim

To show that our names are important to God. He knows us by name, and we are very special to him.

Equipment

None required!

Outline

Introduction

Start by saying that having a good name is very important. Mention that apparently there was once a singer called Reginald Dwight, but his manager felt that it wasn't a good name and he needed to change it. Reginald had two friends in his band – one called Elton and one called John. So he changed his name to a better name – Elton John.

Quiz

Explain that like Elton John, all stars think it is important to have a good name. Split the group into two teams and play the 'famous name' quiz. You may need to give a second clue or a hint to help the groups guess the famous person.

1.	To steal some fruit	NICK BERRY
2.	She's not all white	CILLA BLACK
3.	She's a tough woman	LILY SAVAGE
4.	He commits fraud	SEAN CONNERY
5.	Some extra points please	ROGER MOORE
6.	He flies by the seaside	STEVEN SEAGAL
7.	His name has gone off	FOX MULDER
8.	Her name is like your head	DANA SKULLY
9.	Rabbits all like him	JASPER CARROT
10.	She's got a good point	BRITNEY SPEARS
11.	He's not wrong	IAN WRIGHT
12.	He keeps bouncing up and down	JERRY SPRINGER
13.	A powerful type of vegetation	GEORGE BUSH

14.	How much for those ducks?	JACK/VERA DUCKWORTH
15.	His name can be baked on toast	MR BEAN
16.	A big cat lost in the forest	TIGER WOODS
17.	He walks high up	LUKE SKYWALKER
18.	He uses clay a lot	HARRY POTTER
19.	She's full of electricity	SHARON WATTS

Bible bit

Read from the Bible – Isaiah 43:1-4: 'I called you by name and you are mine.' Encourage the group to believe that they are special to God. Explain that every single name is important to God. He knows everything about everyone sitting here.

Conclusion

Mention that not only is having a good name important, but EVERY single name has a meaning as well, and read out some of the name meanings below. Give some more name meanings if you know any, or have a name book and say that you mean so much to God he loves you more than anyone else.

CHRISTOPHER	Bearing Christ
JOHN	The Lord is gracious
ANDREW	Manly
PETER	The rock
ALICE/ALISON	Nobility
CLAIRE	Clear
KATHERINE	Pure
LAURA	Victory
RACHEL	Gentle, innocent
ROBERT	Bright, famous
BENJAMIN	Son of the right hand
PHILIP	Lover of horses
DAVID	Beloved
SAMANTHA	Heard by God
ELIZABETH	God has promised
LUCY	Light
ALEX	The helper of mankind
KELLY	Warrior maid
JESSICA	The rich one
JOSHUA	God's salvation

Dear Lord . . .

Aim

To show that we may experience problems in life but that God has got all the answers. If we put our trust in him he will answer our prayers.

Equipment

A Bible

Outline

Introduction

Explain that sometimes we experience problems in life, and may question why God allows us to go through these times.

Bible bit

Tell the story of Jonah who ran away from God and boarded a ship – there was a terrible storm and he thought the ship was going to sink – then he was thrown overboard. He thought he would drown, and finally a whale swallowed him whole. He was actually inside the whale's belly and he thought he would be crushed or die slowly – so he prayed. The whale spat him out – he was alive, he did what God told him to do and amazing things happened!

Drama

Explain how important prayer is and ask three people to come straight on to the stage and do the drama 'Dear Lord . . .'

Three people about to pray standing next to each other: Cynic (C), Faithful (F) and Over-the-top (O).

F Dear Lord . . .

C What do you mean 'Dear Lord'? You sound like a right twit, 'Dearest Lord . . .'

F Well he's very dear to me – a great friend indeed.

O You should have said amazing, powerful, generous Lord.

F Look, can I pray?

O Go on then.

ASSEMBLY RESCUE SERVICE

C Do you really have to?

F Dear Lord, please help me, I need to know what to do in this situation. I . . .

C Boring, you only pray when things go wrong. What a waste of time – he can't help you.

F He can – he says to pray in all situations.

C Yeah, and what about when you prayed for your Gran – she died.

F But he has answered some prayers.

C Yeah, you prayed for your cat who was ill.

F And he got better.

C Oh yes – he got knocked down a week later.

O Lord, won't you buy me a Mercedes Benz.

C What're you on? Like God's going to give you one of them.

F Why a Mercedes? Why not a Mini – just as good.

O I can't be seen in a Mini, I've got a reputation to keep.

F But you live two miles from your work, one mile from your mates, one mile from . . .

O I need a car and I want a Merc, so I'll pray.

C God can walk on water and feed 5000 on a tin of tuna and a baguette but he can't give you a Merc!

F I suppose if it's his will. Anyway, my mate's got this really big problem and I need to pray for him. Dear Lord . . .

O I want to win that free holiday to the Bahamas.

F Oh.

C I wonder if God could give me next week's lottery numbers. Nah, load of rubbish.

F God will bless you if it's right and his will.

O Will he give me a free holiday to the Bahamas?

F What's wrong with Skeggy?

C Well, God wouldn't be seen there.

F Can I just pray for my mate? He really needs . . .

O A Mercedes?

F NO.

O A holiday to the Bahamas?

F NO.

C I might ask God for a million pounds, you never know . . .

O Now you're talking. What I could do with a million pounds.

F I need some money for books and I know God provides for all my needs – he's a great God.

C When he's around.

O A million pounds, hey, wow, go on Lord, that would help me in my faith – Mercedes, millions, Bahamas.

F God's always helping you. You've got everything you need – in plenty.

C Ah, but look at the problems in the world – and that miserable couple at No 20. I had to give the bloke a black eye. Where was God, eh, when I needed him?

F Ask him to help you to love them.

O Love them, I'd love a new house as well.

F God, help us to trust you when we need help, and thank you that you have all the answers.

O I still want a Mercedes Benz!

The answer is . . .

Ask for two or three volunteers to come to the front and give them the maths question below. (If they do their maths right, they will always get the same answer as you, no matter what number they choose.)

Pick any number between 1 and 100 (don't tell anyone your number).

- Double it
- Add 30
- Divide it by 2
- Take away the original number

The answer is 15 every time.

Conclusion

End by saying that so many people find prayer a help in times of trouble; no matter how bad a situation may seem, Christians believe God has all the answers.

Trust

Aim

To show the importance of being trustworthy in all situations, and how we can always trust in God – he won't let us down.

Equipment

Two rows of chairs set out
Two blindfolds
A bag of crisps
A tin of custard or beans full of dirt, stones and rubbish
A teaspoon

Outline

Introduction

Start by producing the tin of custard and a spoon and ask the group if anyone likes custard. As the volunteer takes the spoon and is just about to put it in the custard, ask the group if they think you are trustworthy. Let the volunteer get a spoonful of custard, and stop them from eating it! Explain that they trusted you and believed that they were going to get custard, but under the custard was a whole load of dirt, stones from the garden, and rubbish.

Thank the volunteer for trusting you, but say that some people are not trustworthy, and may let you down. Friends may fall out with you, break promises and sometimes do things that hurt or upset you. Explain that we need to be trustworthy in life.

Illustrations

Mention that every day we have to trust in people we never see. Produce the bag of crisps. Say that we don't know under what conditions these crisps are packed. The people who packed them may have dropped some of the crisps on the floor, picked their noses, or gone to the toilet and not washed their hands – but we have to trust that they have been hygienic.

Ask for four volunteers. Blindfold two of them and tell the other two that they are to be the 'guides'. The two guides have to guide the two blindfolded volunteers across the chairs stepping from one chair to the next by giving them instructions such as, one step to the right, one to the left. (Make sure that you are next to the volunteers just to ensure their safety.) Afterwards read out the poems 'Alone' and 'Heartache'.

Alone

When you don't know where to turn to,
> when no one seems to care,
> turn to face Christ Jesus
> and leave your worries there.

His love will never fail you,
> he knows your every need,
> he only does what's best for you,
> just follow where he leads.

Heartache

At times I feel so distant,
> I don't know where to turn,
> but you, my Lord, are waiting,
> to take me in your arms.

I know how much you love me,
> I know how much you care.
I only have you to turn to
> when I'm in deep despair.

You wipe away the tears,
> you take away the pain.
You fill my heart with peace and joy,
> you make me whole again.

Conclusion

Finish by saying that in the game, the two 'blind' volunteers had no idea what lay ahead of them. They could have fallen and broken their necks, but they had to trust in the guides who led them to safety across the chairs.

As in the two poems, we may not be able to physically see God, but if we put our trust in him and follow him he will guide us safely through life and never let us down.

Fears

Aim

To show that we all have fears at different times in our lives. Our fears may start off small, but can become dominant and overwhelming. God can help us through our fears though, if we put our trust in him.

Equipment

Any piece of juggling equipment such as small and large juggling balls, rings or clubs.
A Bible

Outline

Introduction

Start off by juggling with one or two small juggling balls, or ask for volunteers to have a go. Explain that this is the basic equipment used for juggling. Then juggle with some larger balls. Finally pick up a piece of juggling equipment, such as a club, and say that juggling starts off small (show the balls) but you need to go onto bigger things to look impressive. Ask for a volunteer to have a go and then do it yourself.

Relate juggling to fear in that it starts off small, like the balls, but then if we allow fear to take hold, it can become worse. Explain that there are many different sorts of fear that people suffer from.

Game

Play 'Guess the fear'. Read out some of the different fears and people have to guess what the fear is.

- Aquaphobia is the fear of WATER
- Aerophobia is the fear of FLYING
- Hypsophobia is the fear of HEIGHTS
- Aracnophobia is the fear of SPIDERS
- Brontophobia is the fear of THUNDERSTORMS
- Decidophobia is the fear of MAKING DECISIONS

- Pyrophobia is the fear of FIRE
- Ailurophobia is the fear of CATS
- Gynephobia is the fear of WOMEN
- Hippophobia is the fear of HORSES
- Ochlophobia is the fear of CROWDS
- Xenophobia is the fear of STRANGERS
- Anthropophobia is the fear of PEOPLE

Tell a story of when you've had a scary experience in life.

Bible bit

Read out Isaiah 43:1-5, which talks about God's love and his help in times of fear.

Conclusion

End by saying that God loves us and if we ask him to take away our fears he may help us to overcome them, look after us, and give us peace.

Advice

Aim

To encourage the group to realise that when people give them advice it is usually for their safety and well being, and not to dismiss it but to think about the advice they are given in life.

Equipment

A bar of chocolate (prize)
A recently bought product from a shop, preferably electrical

Outline

Introduction

Hold up a product that you've recently bought (preferably an electrical one) and explain that whenever you buy a product from a shop there is always a safety advice label on it. Sometimes this safety advice is very important, but sometimes it's really daft. Read out the daft safety advice below:

- Do not use your hands to stop the chain – on a chainsaw.
- Keep the bottle upright after opening – on a flavoured-milk bottle.
- Do not iron clothes whilst on your body – on an electric iron.
- Do not light the flame near your face – on a cigarette lighter.
- The image you can see is behind you – on a rear-view mirror.
- The pudding will be hot after heating – on a bread-and-butter pudding.
- Do not turn the dessert upside down – on the bottom of the container.
- Contains nuts – on a packet of peanuts.
- The patient should not drive a car or operate machinery and should avoid alcohol – on cough syrup for toddlers.
- Warning: may cause drowsiness – on medicine sold to insomniacs.
- Functional only when there is a film inside – on a camera sold in Europe.
- This item is not to be used as a life preserver or swimming aid – on a joke inflatable saxophone.
- Keep out of children – on a Korean kitchen knife.
- Only works in sub-zero temperatures – on a de-icing spray.

Illustration

Explain that sometimes we get advice from different people in life and think it is daft and irrelevant, just as the safety advice you have just read out. Read out or show on an OHP the 'vacuum flask' sheet. Mention that in the same way the advice we get from people can seem over the top and too burdensome.

Vacuum flask

For best use and care results please read the following information.

Initial use

- Ensure that the inside of your flask is cleaned with warm water/washing up liquid solution and thoroughly rinsed before first use, or if the flask has been used for a period of time.
- Do not immerse completely in water.

Cleaning

- After each use wash your flask as above and store with the stopper off to allow it to dry fully inside and prevent residual odours.
- Do not clean your flask in a dishwasher.
- Remove stubborn stains by soaking with a solution of bicarbonate of soda in hot water. Rinse fully afterwards.
- Do not use abrasive cleaners, solvents or bleach.

Care in use

- For best performance, pre-fill your flask with warm water before storing hot drinks, or cold water for cold/chilled drinks.
- Do not overfill your flask, fill to approximately 10 mm below the top of the inner liquid holder to allow space for the stopper.
- Ensure that the stopper and cup are fully tightened.
- This flask is intended for table-top use only.

Flask easy-pour system

- To pour from the flask, turn the stopper – turn in a counter-clockwise direction and tip the flask with the spout facing forward. Alternatively, remove the stopper completely. This is recommended when fruits or vegetables are present in the drink.

Caution

- Your flask includes some plastic parts. Keep away from sources of direct heat to prevent damage.
- Do not store carbonated (fizzy) drinks or dry ice in your flask as the build up of gas may forcefully eject the stopper.

- Do not store warm milk or baby food in your flask as this may lead to bacterial growth.
- Drink from the cup supplied and not directly from the flask.
- The inner part of this flask is a fragile glass container.
- Due to the fragility of the inner container we do not recommend the use of solid or frozen objects or ice cubes.

Game

Ask for about 10 volunteers and play 'Simon says'. The aim of the game is for you to give them a command, but they are only allowed to obey if you have said 'Simon says' (or your own name). If they do something 'Simon' hasn't said, they are out. Give a prize to the winner.

Conclusion

End by saying that as in the game, if we do our own thing in life we may lose out, but if we follow the right advice, we may be more successful. The advice we get may seem daft or over the top, but it is always there for our safety and well-being. Encourage the group to listen to advice from parents or teachers, weigh it up and if they still think it's no good – OK – but give them a chance.

Cars

Aim

To show that material possessions, wealth and self-fulfilment won't always give us real satisfaction, or true happiness – only Jesus can – and when we go through sad or difficult times God can help us if we put our trust in him.

Equipment

Sketchboard
Marker pens

Outline

Introduction

Say that one of the most annoying things ever is when your car doesn't start in the morning!

Give a funny illustration of when you've had a breakdown on a journey, seen one, or read about one. Afterwards read out the sketch below.

My car

I was driving along in my car one day when I saw loads of people staring at me. I asked them what they were staring at. They said that they couldn't believe that anyone would drive such an old banger – 'Well,' I replied, 'you might be wondering AUDI you drive an old banger. Well, you don't have to worry about CITROEN comfortably, but maybe I'm DAF or just too CAVALIER to care, but I reckon it's no MINOR feat to drive an old banger. You might think that to get into this car you'll be CORTINA trap (DATSUN other one) but I reckon that this car is a TRIUMPH for me; but if it makes you laugh, OK, you can ROLLS HONDA floor laughing, pleading for MERCEDES if you like.

'OK, so it makes a lot of noise; when I drive home the neighbours shout "VAUXHALL that noise about? If the noise gets any LADA I'll set my ROVER on to you!" I think to myself I'd like to give them a kick up the ASTRA. I hate people who complain about my car, UNO what I mean? Well, what an ESTATE to get into. They're always going loopy about my car; one day somebody'll probably ESCORT them to the loony bin, shouting, "SIERRA mechanic anywhere?"

'Well, I don't think I could a FORD a PORSCHE car, just this JEEP one. Well, they're always ROBIN you of money. I don't need a car to PANDA me.

'Anyway, I don't think I can FIAT any more jokes in this MINI sketch, so I'll say "That's all, VOLKS".'

Yours, MORRIS.

Sketchboard

Write on the Sketchboard the word 'Cars'. Say that often people misuse cars for various reasons. Then write down the following words and explanations:

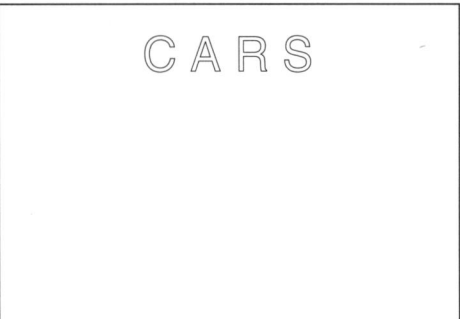

Joyriding – stealing a car and driving for a bit of fun

Speed – fast driving, and not worrying about the dangers

Ram-raiding – using a car to knock through a wall to steal something

Status – having the best car is important for street cred

Get-away – being able to get away as quickly as possible from the Police

Relate these things to people, and how they try to fill their lives with different things to make them happy.

JOYRIDING – for some people life can be one long 'joy' ride – a good career, wealth, possessions, the good things in life. But this doesn't guarantee REAL satisfaction or happiness.

SPEED – some people, especially young people, see the way to fulfilment in life as 'living life in the fast lane' – taking drugs, alcohol, having sex, etc. But these things don't always bring REAL happiness.

STATUS – having respect and success or having street cred may be good, but it may not last.

RAM-RAIDING – perhaps the way to be happy is to go through life like a ram-raider – knocking anything or anyone that's in your way out of the way. Nothing can stop you doing what you want to do in life. No problem is too big, you're in control. This doesn't guarantee that you can cope when you have problems in life.

GET-AWAY – sometimes we say, 'I'll do my own thing, seek a fast get-away from the rat race, seek religion, or be at one with myself' . . . this may be good for a short while but does not guarantee true happiness.

BUT...

Christians believe that if we put our trust in Jesus he'll give us total satisfaction – meaning and purpose to our life.

Finally, go back to the word 'Cars' on the sketchboard and mention that all cars 'break down' at some point. Fill in the words and then say that when that happens you know 'a man who can', 'a nice man, a very, very nice man' who knows every detail about your car and has it fixed within a few minutes – amazing!

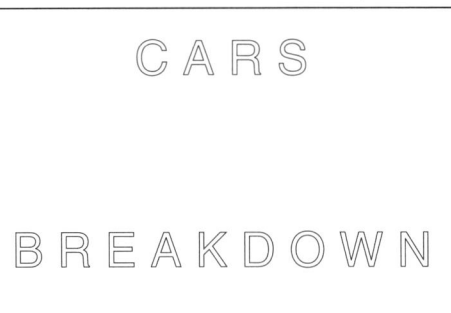

Explain that in the same way we all have certain problems at some stage in our lives. It may be problems with our 'bodywork' or external problems but there is 'a nice man, a very, very nice man' who can help us.

Conclusion

Jesus knows everything about us, yet he still loves us. If we put our trust in him, as with the rescue services, he can get us started again by helping us through our problems or fixing the problem for us.

Ziggy

Aim

To show that being rich and looking for satisfaction in this world doesn't always make you happy, but if you put your trust in Jesus he can give you life in all its fullness. Also, when we do wrong, if we ask for God's forgiveness, he can forgive us, because of Christ's death on the cross.

Equipment

As much juggling equipment as you have (balls, clubs, rings, etc.)
As many magic tricks as you have

Outline

Introduction

Produce a wad of money (or monopoly money) and ask if anyone wants it. Talk about people who won the National Lottery then realised that money and possessions didn't always bring happiness.

Story

Tell a short story or give a quote from someone famous who's got loads of money, but aren't happy. Otherwise tell the story of 'Zacchaeus' from the Bible.

Drama

Perform the drama 'Ziggy' (based on the parable of the Lost Son – Luke 15:11-24). You need to be able to juggle a bit and do a few magic tricks to do this.

Characters: **N**: Narrator; **Z**: Ziggy

N Once upon a time there was a young lad called Ziggy Oswald Gazebo, otherwise known as 'Ziggy'. You might think that he had a funny name. Well, you're right, he did. You see, his family were all circus entertainers. His mum and dad were trapeze artists, and his brother was a lion-tamer. As for Ziggy, he just did a bit of juggling.

Do some juggling

N But Ziggy wasn't very good, as he didn't get much time to practise. You see, everybody had a job to do in the circus, but he had the worst job of all:

Mime

He cleaned up the lion dung . . . and the camel dung . . .

In fact, Ziggy cleaned up all the dung!!

He was fed up; all he wanted to do was entertain people.

Do a magic or juggling trick

N But the only spectators he had were the ANIMALS, and they weren't very impressed.

Ziggy had everything he needed, but he wasn't happy, he wanted more. He thought to himself:

Z I'm fed up with life. I want as many things as money can buy. After all, I have my whole life ahead of me, I wonder if I can split with my family . . . ?

Do an illusion that splits things, if you have one.

Z Yes I can! I will! I'm going to go to my father and ask him for MY share of the inheritance, all that he has for me. After all, that money will be mine one day. Well, I want it now. Then I can go off to a distant land and live it up, enjoy myself, have fun, yeah, money, money, money . . .

N So Ziggy went to his father and asked him for his share of the money.

Mime Ziggy asking his father for the money

N Sadly, Ziggy's father agreed to give him all the money. Ziggy was really happy, he'd never seen so much money! *(which he puts into a magic bag)*. Straight-away he set off for a distant land.

When he was there he made loads of friends and he entertained them with his tricks.

Do a juggling or magic trick

N He gave away his money, on interest of course!! And he spent his money . . .

Juggle (with visual aids, and in different ways) or mime

N He joined the local Tennis Club *(tennis ball)*

And a Football Club *(football)*

He had his own business, but he was a bit underhand *(juggle underhand)*

He was always swapping cars *(toy cars)*

His life was all over the place *(throw balls in air)*

As for Ziggy, he was up and down, up and down *(columns)*

Wherever there was money he followed it like a . . . *(yo-yo)*

He often went out clubbing *(juggle clubs)*

Once there he met lots of girls

He would buy them expensive rings *(juggling rings)*

N Sadly, Ziggy's life was empty; he tried to fill it with things to make him happy, but still his life was empty...

Magic trick (disappearing and reappearing trick)

N Eventually he went out to get some more money – it was gone! He lost his friends, his business, his house, in fact, he lost everything! So he looked for a job. Eventually he found one. But it wasn't very good; he only did it to make money:

Mime

Cleaning at the local pig farm. He had to clean out all the pigs. Did it smell or what! He was so hungry he tried to eat the food that the pigs had left, the food that had been trampled and messed on by the pigs!!

N Eventually, he came to his senses. He thought to himself,

Z I've been really selfish, greedy and bad. I'm going to go back to my father and apologise to him. I'll ask him if he'll take me back on as a hired servant. I'm not worthy to be his son.

N So Ziggy started walking back home. After a while he noticed a figure in the distance... a No. 8 bus! Then he noticed another figure... his father. Quickly he ran up to his father, knelt down and said:

Z Father, I've been really bad. I wasted all the money that you gave me on reckless living. Please forgive me, and take me back on as one of your hired servants, as I'm not worthy to be your son.

N His father hugged him and said:

MY SON, I THOUGHT YOU WERE LOST... BUT NOW YOU'RE FOUND! I THOUGHT YOU WERE DEAD... BUT YOU'RE ALIVE! WELCOME HOME SON...
OH, BY THE WAY, DO YOU KNOW ANYONE WHO WANTS A JOB IN A CIRCUS... AS A CLOWN!

Conclusion

End by talking about God's forgiveness, through Christ's death and resurrection, and how only God can give us life in its fullness.

This world

Aim

To show how beautiful the world is, yet so often we misuse it for our own selfish desires and are slowly destroying it. We need to look after God's planet.

Equipment

'Classic ad' tape (Available from most record shops)
World resources facts
Products from a supermarket

Outline

Play a piece of classical music for half a minute. Afterwards explain how beautiful classical music is and how so often it is used on TV to advertise different products.

Game

Play 'Guess the ad'. Choose two volunteers then play a piece of classical music which is used on TV to advertise a product. The two volunteers have to try to guess from the products on the table (or a written list) which product is associated with that particular piece of music.

Explain that, sadly, the music that was created years ago for people's pleasure has now been misused, as it is now used just to encourage people to spend lots of money on products such as cars, bread, or motor oil. Show some of the products used in the adverts from which you have just played the music.

Illustrations

Produce a flower or a picture of a tree and say how beautiful the world is in which we live. God created it for our pleasure, and yet like the classical music it has been misused to our own advantage, often without thinking of the consequences.

Read out some facts about the world's resources (available from the Internet, libraries or bookshops).

Conclusion

End by giving examples of what we can do to look after the world, such as putting litter into bins, saving items for recycling, or using environmentally friendly products.

Finish with the following Cree Indian prophecy:

'Only after the last tree has been cut down,
only after the last river has been poisoned,
only after the last fish has been caught,
only then will you find that money cannot be eaten.'

Harvest

Aim

To encourage the group to be thankful to God for what they've got. To understand that some people in life are less privileged than ourselves, and think of ways in which we can help those who are in need.

Equipment

Three pots of yoghurt, three spoons, three blindfolds
A bowl of cereal

Outline

Introduction

Start by asking the group to put up their hands if they haven't had breakfast this morning. If someone hasn't, offer them the bowl of cereal and let them eat it. Say how privileged we are. Most of us have had a nice breakfast, we aren't starving.

Games

Play the game 'Word association'. Ask for two volunteers to come forward and give them the word 'food'. As one of them says 'food' the other has to say a word which relates to that and so on. Emphasise how much we have and ask the group to be thankful for all we have!!

Choose six volunteers. Give three of them a pot of yoghurt and a spoon each and then blindfold them. They need to stand up. Ask the other three to sit down on chairs in front of those three. Put blankets over them up to their chins, and make sure each blindfolded volunteer has a volunteer directly in front of them. On the word 'go' the three blindfolded volunteers have to feed the yoghurt to the partner in front of them.

The winner is the person to have emptied their yoghurt pot.

Explain that the volunteers who were fed the yoghurts had no control; they couldn't use their hands, so they were at the mercy of their 'feeders'. Some people in life are in the same situation. They may be restricted either physically or financially and not enjoy the same pleasures in life that we all take for granted. We need to try and understand people who are in need, such as those who are starving or homeless.

Making a difference
There's a world out there dying to know –
    who can help them? where can they go?
Death, destruction, hopelessness, fears,
    emptiness, hunger, sadness and tears.

Take some pills, drink and smoke,
    fun and pleasure, what a joke.
Forget your problems, they'll go away,
    funny, that's what the comfortable say.

Does anyone care? – not at all?
People watch their step so they don't fall,
    look at society, too busy to care,
    they look after themselves, just sit and stare.

Just worry about yourself, money and life issues.
It makes us so sad, we reach for our tissues,
    no time for us, what do we matter,
    so long as your wages get fatter and fatter.

Just once a year you can take the lead,
    and throw some money at Children In Need,
    then you've done your bit until next year,
    when you're asked for more – say no fear.

But is that enough? Just money won't do,
    what we want is more of you.
The one thing that matters when push comes to shove,
    we don't just want money, we want more and more love.

Please help those who need it
    with money and time,
    then I won't need to write
    this daft silly rhyme.

Conclusion
End by saying that when we help other people, as in the yoghurt game, we can have fun. Give some examples of organisations that need help, such as projects that

work with those from the developing world, the homeless, or local organisations or projects which need some help!

Ask the group to think of fun creative ways to help people – not just by giving financially, but by actually getting involved, such as a sponsored event.

Mothers...

Aim

To show that mothers are special. They often work very hard for our benefit, and really care for us. Mother's Day is an important day, as it's an opportunity for us to show our thanks to our mums.

Equipment

Poster – if you can get hold of one, the poster that looks like an old woman until you turn it upside down, when it becomes a young woman.

Outline

Start by asking the group what special day is coming up. Explain that it's Mother's Day, and for one day they have to treat their mum as if she was famous.

Quiz

Ask for 2 volunteers to do the quiz 'Guess the famous mum'. Give them a few clues and get the rest of the group to help out. Some famous mums could be:

Queen Mother

Mother Hubbard

Mother Goose

Mary, the mother of Jesus

Old woman in shoe (so many children)

Peggy Mitchell

Include any famous TV personalities who have just had babies.

Talk about our attitudes towards our mums, and how often we take them for granted without realising that they really care for us, and do so much for us. Afterwards perform the following rap.

My mum ... aaahh

I lie in bed, no cares at all,
    peace right now, then I hear her squall.

MOTHERS...

Get up, she says, wash and dress,
    comb your hair, it's all a mess.
You have five minutes till breakfast time,
    if you don't, your toast is mine.
Toast well done, scrape the burn,
    wash up, she says, it's your turn.

Oh that woman, she nags me so
    but she's my mum and I love her though.

Tidy your room, she would say,
    put those magazines away.
Make your bed, keep it neat
    put your shoes on your feet.
CDs, megadrives everywhere,
    your room's a tip, don't you care?
Put your school books in your bag.
Oh that woman, what a nag.
Do this, do that, she would say
    or you're grounded on Monday.

Oh that woman, she nags me so
    but she's my mum and I love her though.

A trip with school, a week away.
I can't wait for that day –
    no more chores or work to do,
    loads of fun and freedom too!!
When I get there I realise,
    without my mum it isn't too nice;
    I'm too selfish, I can't see
    that my mum really cares for me.
My mum is great, she's first-rate.
Packs my bags, makes my food
    I wish I wasn't really rude.
She sees me off, looks after me,
    gives me treats for my tea.
There's one thing that I know:
    my mum really loves me so.

Oh that woman, she nags me so
    but she's my mum and I love her though.

In my life when I've been scared,
    I've always known my mum cared.
She does so much and works so hard,
    I love her, so I'll get her a card.

Conclusion

End by showing the old/young woman poster, and explain that we should realise that our mums are very special. Whilst we are children they may seem like the 'old' woman sometimes, always nagging us or misunderstanding us, but really they may be like the 'young' woman: kind, special and loving. Most important of all, let's take this opportunity to thank them, and show them our love on Mother's Day.

The cost of love

Aim

To show that the greatest sacrifice that we can make is to lay down our lives to save other people. This is a very hard thing to do, yet requires one thing – love. Whilst it may be hard, having real love for others can be achieved.

Equipment

A current pop song about love

Outline

Introduction

Start by talking about one of the worst jobs that people can do: being a bodyguard (or talk about a recent film with a bodyguard in it). Explain what it would be like to face death every day through possible assassination attempts.

Illustration

Read out a newspaper article about someone who has done something really heroic and saved someone's life. A good example of a hero is Andrew Parker, otherwise known as 'The Human Bridge', who saved many lives on the Herald of Free Enterprise (Zeebrugge disaster) by lying across a sheer drop, enabling the passengers to walk across him to safety.

Talk about other people who, for one reason or another, were willing to face death to save lives. A lot of people would walk away, or fight to save their own life. Yet these people didn't. They had one thing that enabled them to do what they did – love for others.

Song

Play the song about love that you chose. Afterwards, read out the poem below.

The Love of Christ
As I stand beneath the cross
    I look into your eyes,
    I see the pain and agony,
    I hear your piercing cries.

Lord, I'll never understand
    just why you died for me,
    the anguish and the torment
    as you hung upon the tree.

Lord, I bow before you,
    at your feet I humbly fall,
    I am so unworthy
    but still you gave your all.

You crown me with your glory,
    you robe me in your love,
    you tell me I am special
    that's why you gave your blood.

Conclusion

End by saying that we should love one another if we want to see a better world, but how far does our love stretch? Explain that the meaning of Easter is about Jesus, and how he was prepared to lay down his life to save us from death.

All smashed up

Aim

To show that the real meaning of Easter is that Christ died for our mistakes, so that we could be forgiven. Also three days later he rose from the dead.

Equipment

An old tie
A pair of scissors
A hammer
A Mars bar™
A snazzy box or bag
One bath towel
An old ornament
Glue
A Bible

Outline

Before taking the assembly (or the afternoon before) give a member of staff an old tie to wear for the assembly, and ask them to play along with the trick.

Introduction
Start by telling the group that you have a new trick to perform. Produce the bag or box. Ask for a member of staff (the volunteer) to come forward and lend their tie. Explain that you are going to cut through the tie, drop it into the box and say the magic words. When you lift out the tie again it will be perfect – no cut. With bated breath, then cut the tie, drop it into the box (the volunteer teacher should be looking worried – good acting would help). Produce the tie – it's ruined. The teacher is very unhappy!! The kids think that you've gone wrong – say sorry and look very worried.

Explain that you've made a big mistake, you've really messed up, and say that as we approach Easter we think about how Jesus died on the cross 2000 years ago for our mistakes so that we can be forgiven and become his followers.

Bible bit

Read out Matthew 27:45-54 which explains about Christ's death.

Illustration

If you can get away with it a second time, pretend that you've got another new trick and produce the ornament. Show the group how lovely it is, then cover it with the towel and say that you are going to smash it with the hammer, and it will still be in one piece. Bang the hammer on it. Show the group the smashed ornament. Then produce the Mars bar and the glue. Say that if anyone can make it perfect just like it was before, they win the Mars bar. There won't be any volunteers who can do this.

Conclusion

Finish by saying that Christ was crucified – he was dead, broken beyond all hope, like the ornament. He was put in the tomb with a stone weighing between one and one-and-a-half tonnes rolled across and a Roman guard in front (at least four soldiers), and yet three days later amazingly he was seen by approximately 500 people alive and well, risen again. This is what Easter is all about.

Stuff the turkey

Aim

To encourage the group to think about people who are suffering, especially at Christmas time, and think of ways to help them.

Equipment

A pack of mince pies
A flipchart

Outline

Introduction
Split the group into two teams and ask for a volunteer from each team. The two volunteers have one minute to write on the flipchart as many things as possible that relate to the word 'Christmas' (their group can help by shouting things out). See which volunteer has written the most things down.

Explain how great Christmas is, but for a lot of people Christmas is just about parties, food and drink. We fill ourselves up with loads of food such as turkey, mince pies and Christmas pudding.

Choose two more volunteers and give them a minute to see who can eat the most mince pies. Afterwards, read out the poem below.

Stuff the turkey
Stuff the turkey, be stuffed with food,
    this Christmas, it's party mood.
Get a present from your guest,
    I want the best so stuff the rest.

It's Christmas shopping, one great big panic,
    thousands of people all going manic.
People, people everywhere,
    looking for presents, they don't care.
One shop entrance all rush through,
    a little old lady pushes you.

Little kids meek and mild,
   it's his parents going wild.

Christmas party, loads of fun,
   food and drink for everyone.
Have as much as you can take
   till you puke from drink and cake.
People jumping, non-stop pleasure,
   whatever's fun there's no measure.

Christmas Day, family round,
   laughter and cheer the only sound.
Open the present, shout with joy,
   you've got the latest trendy toy.
It's turkey, stuffing, the full works we've got,
   mince pies and cake, the whole lot.

Full your belly, then put on the telly,
   soaps, dramas, films old and new,
   then the Queen's speech we listen to.
Too stuffed to move so pass the wine,
   I love this Christmas, it's really fine.

Stuff the turkey, be stuffed with food,
   this Christmas, it's party mood.
Get a present from your guest –
   I want the best so stuff the rest.

Cold and drizzly, nowhere to go,
   on the pavement lies old Joe.
No family, friends or food for him,
   his only present, a bottle of gin.
Will he live, will he die,
   'Who cares?' he says with a sigh.

'Where's my mummy?' Jane will shout.
   'Shut up you idiot, or you're out!'
No family, no presents, no love for Jane,
   only a long, hurtful pain.
'I wish I wasn't at this place,' she says
   with tears rolling – her life's a mess.

Stuff the turkey, be stuffed with food,
    this Christmas it's party mood.
Get a present from your guest –
    I want the best so stuff the rest.

Conclusion

End by saying that this Christmas we need to think about other people who are less fortunate than us, and suggest ways in which we can help, such as putting money into collection boxes, sending a Christmas card or present to someone you wouldn't normally send one to, and being nice to each other.

The reason for the season

Aim

The aim is to show that in many ways the true meaning of Christmas has been forgotten. For a lot of people Christmas is just about Christmas shopping and receiving presents. The true meaning is that Jesus Christ was born on the earth as the Saviour of the world. He was God's present to us.

Equipment

Three ordinary objects
Three sheets of Christmas wrapping paper
Some sellotape and scissors
Three blindfolds

Outline

Introduction

Begin by saying that Christmas is meant to be a very special event yet in many ways it has been exploited commercially. For a lot of people it's all about shopping and buying and receiving presents. Whilst this is nice, it can create greed and selfishness, and can put financial pressure on people, making Christmas a very sad event, instead of a celebration of Christ's birth.

Read out the sketch below and ask the group to count how many names of shops they can recognise. Give a prize for the person who gets the right amount.

Be wise and select

Christmas, what's it about? That one major event you do every year – you guessed it, Christmas shopping! So many shops to visit, so many presents to buy. What do you get? Which shops do you go to?

I need an INDEX to find out. Instead of going to every shop I need to SELECT the right one, and not spend so much money. I need a KWIK SAVE, but ALDI save money at Christmas. Well, I need to work out OUR PRICE and look for the right present, but it ASDA be cheap. I need to BE WISE, money doesn't go far – unless you got a POUND STRETCHER. Cheap presents, that's the SAFEWAY to shop.

I know, I'll take four friends with me: DOROTHY PERKINS and LAURA ASHLEY, they'll do, they're TOP GIRLS, and I'll call for MORRISONS and JONATHON JAMES; they'll be CO-OPERATIVE and help me out.

So off we went. We started at LITTLEWOODS, that was Dorothy's FIRST CHOICE, but it didn't take long to go through. 'Where NEXT?' we thought. TESCO to BHS and buy something: a shirt for my brother, my sister likes to be seen in BOOTS and my mother, anything at all – what does MOTHERCARE? Gran, she likes knitting, something to knit. How much is WOOLWORTH? For Baby Jim a new bib, he's always getting his dirty; we need to buy one you can MARK 1 and wipe clean. EVANS knows what we can buy Dad. ATHENA nice watch he'd like.

We've almost finished, full MARKS to us, but we've SPENCER packet already. Let's go for BURTON. I'm hungry, who likes CURRIES? Or do you prefer RATNER tui? In the end we H. SAMUELS *(ate some meals)* in the High Street. So off we went, and bumped straight into Donald SIMPSON'S trolley, and I spilled my cola over him. 'Sorry about that,' I said after I'd McDONALD'S shirt up. Then ARGOS and puts my foot in it, 'How's your girlfriend?' He looked quite sad: 'I MISS SELFRIDGE a lot, we're not PARTNERS any more, she's left me.' I felt sorry for him, he's a TOP MAN. He lives in a SWISS COTTAGE in Hackney. We left him and met my friend RICHARDS, he's from a RIVER ISLAND in KENTUCKY, TEXAS. He's just bought a PIZZALAND in SALISBURY to build his own ranch on.

'I'm tired, where can my BODYSHOP next?' I asked the other four. They replied, 'What a WIMPEY'.

Christmas shopping, don't just get a bit at a time! DO IT ALL– *NOW!*

Game
Explain that when you've done the Christmas shopping you need to wrap the presents up, and play the game 'Wrap up'. For this you need three volunteers. They have to wrap up three different objects in wrapping paper as quick and tidy as possible, blindfolded!

Conclusion
End by saying that sadly, for a lot of people, Christmas is just about buying and receiving presents. This can create greed and selfishness. Very often the true meaning about Christmas is forgotten. Christmas is about Jesus. He is God's son who came down to earth and lived as a man. As with the presents, his birth wasn't particularly special on the outside, he was born as a normal baby in a dirty old stable, not a palace. He was visited by a few shepherds, not by thousands of Kings, Queens, Princes or leaders, yet he is special – he was born to be the Saviour of the World. That's what Christmas is all about.

Can you believe it?

Aim

To show that the real meaning of Christmas is Christ's birth and that we need to believe in him.

Equipment

Some dressing-up equipment
A bottle of lemonade and two glasses

Outline

Introduction

Start by holding up a variety pack of 50 Christmas cards and ask the group what pictures they think are on the cards. Explain that out of the whole pack of 50 there are likely to be only 1 or 2 pictures of the Nativity – yet this is what Christmas is meant to be all about.

Drama

Ask for some volunteers and act out the Nativity story off the cuff. Afterwards read out the poem below. Then explain that Christmas is all about Christ's birth and we need to believe in him.

Can you believe it?

Jesus Christ – born in a stable,
    was it true or was it a fable?
Bright star and angels, shepherds and kings,
    so the old choir always sings.
Unto us a child is born,
    ding dong, merrily on high,
    we all sing at Christmas time – with a heavy sigh.
Such a nice story – yet so long ago.
Was it made up? We don't know.

But can you believe anything in this world today?
Life on Mars is what they say.

Technology, computers, money and power,
> is it a breakthrough, or the world gone sour?

Increase your wealth – it's all about greed,
> but don't we know what is our need.

Man's violence and hatred – all so bad,
> look at the world so lonely and sad.

So we look at the story about the newborn baby
> and think was it true – well maybe.

There was Mary and Joseph, the joy of new birth,
> the greatest event in the history of earth.

Remember this Christmas – it was all there,
> the Saviour was born for the earth's repair.

So we believe and trust in him,
> he's the only true and stable thing.

Game

Split the group into two teams and ask for a volunteer from each team. Give each volunteer a glass of lemonade and the title of a Christmas carol. They have to gurgle the carol and the rest of the team have to guess which carol is being gurgled. When the group have guessed correctly, give them another carol and see who is the winner.

Conclusion

Finish by saying that Christmas is fun, like the game, but not only do we need to remember that it is Jesus' birthday, we need to celebrate it too!

By the same author

ISBN 1 84417 014 4
Catalogue No. 1500564